Metaphor Stories for Hypnosis: Stimulate Change While Telling a Tale

Shawn Marie Howe BSN, CHt

ISBN:1461181593
ISBN-13:978-1461181590

DEDICATION

For David ~
who has always supported me, through thick and thin,
and many, many changes.

Contents

Introduction

Everyone knows about stories. There is hardly any one among us that has not heard, at some point in their lives, those four wonderfully familiar words, "once upon a time…" Many of us are immediately swept back to happy and simpler times in our childhood when we were nurtured and loved and soothed to sleep by stories passed down through the ages.

Metaphor Stories for Hypnosis are very much the same as the stories of our childhood. They have a definite beginning, middle and end, with some positive moral outcome. The metaphors themselves may be obvious or disguised within the story, but make no mistake; the right brain, when appropriately relaxed via a suitable induction, will find the message every time! The familiarity of the story format fosters clients' further relaxation, making the process more comfortable and accessible for them.

Metaphor Stories for Hypnosis: Stimulate Change While Telling a Tale, can be used with many clients, as the stories are fairly general and express universal themes and ideas. Most of them are written in the female voice, because so much of my practice is with women (and that's how I think); but they can just as easily be adapted for use with male clientele. In my practice, I have found it most useful to utilize these stories after the client has been induced to a light to medium trance level and before any specific suggestion work is undertaken. The stories can often act as a deepener, as well. You may choose to use them differently.

I have written the stories using ellipsis marks […] to indicate phrasing and rhythm, but feel free to read them in whatever way is most comfortable and natural for you.

I hope you find *Metaphor Stories for Hypnosis: Stimulate Change While Telling a Tale*, enjoyable and helpful. I welcome comments regarding your individual results. I can be reached at: www.ahealingplacecanby.com.

ONE

AN ORDINARY WOMAN

Once upon a time there was a lovely young woman with soft (brown/blonde) hair and eyes that were gentle like a fawn's and a laugh that flowed like water over pebbles after the rain.

The young woman was not so large and not so small; Not so strong and not so weak; Just an ordinary woman…And she was very blessed because she was also a mother – a mother of a beautiful, adorable, loving, happy baby (girl/boy).

And everyday, this young woman and her infant (daughter/son) would take a walk... all around their neighborhood, all around their town… and wave and smile at everyone they'd meet. Everyone loved them and everyone knew that this young mother was blessed, indeed.

Then one day, while the mother and child were out for their daily stroll, the unexpected happened. The young woman turned to look at something that caught her attention – it doesn't really matter what it was – perhaps it was a kitten in the pet store window…perhaps a bush covered with enticing pink flowers…perhaps a cloud as it skittered across the sun – and in that moment, her tiny (daughter/son) in (her/his) baby stroller, rolled, and rolled, and rolled away from her - faster and faster… farther and farther – and all the time that this was happening the young mother kept thinking – no – hearing inside her head, really – "there's nothing you can do… all is lost… just give in – this is how it is… you are only an ordinary woman."

And for a split second, the lovely young woman, the mother of this precious child… believed the thoughts in her head – why would they lie to her? But then she heard herself scream out loud, "I can do this! I can do whatever I set my mind to!" And she ran, faster than the wind, down hills, across paths, through traffic, after the careening stroller that carried her most precious possession, her infant (daughter/son).

The stroller hit a rock, flew into the air, over the guardrail running alongside the road, and catapulted into the river below. The young woman, who did not know how to swim, never hesitated. She dodged the rock, jumped onto the railing as if it were a diving board, and soared into the air, landing in the cold and streaming water far below.

People who witnessed the event will tell you that she made a beautiful swan-dive into the river, with the look of such determination on her face that a train or a tornado could not have stopped her.

When she hit the water, she grabbed a quick breath and paddled with all fours, as fast and as hard as she could… toward the stroller that held her baby. But the stroller had a head start. It was disappearing downstream quickly – she knew she was tiring fast – and that she would have to reach her baby, now or never.

And then she heard the words inside her head again – "there's nothing you can do…all is lost…just give in – this is how it is...you are just an ordinary woman." She thought about quitting – about just letting the current sweep her away, depositing her wherever it ended – but then she heard herself scream out loud – "NO! I *can* do it! I have the power! Even an ordinary woman can do an extraordinary deed!"

And with that, she sucked in a huge breath of air, put her head down, and tore through the water, reaching out for and grabbing onto the stroller... just as it was about to sink beneath the choppy, blue waves.

She dragged the stroller and herself to the nearest shoreline... climbed out onto the pebbled ground and collapsed. Her baby (daughter/son), whose head had been held afloat because of the stroller's buoyancy, let out a laugh and clapped and clapped and clapped, as if to say "*I knew* you could do it – I knew you could do it all along!"

And people all over town, for years and years, told the tale of the lovely young woman with soft (brown/blonde) hair and eyes that were gentle like a fawn's and a laugh that flowed like water over pebbles after the rain – of the woman who was not so large and not so small; Not so strong and not so weak; Just an ordinary woman – who put her mind to a task that she HAD to accomplish – AND DID!

Even an ordinary woman can do an extraordinary deed.

TWO

THE RETURN OF CHINA ROOSTER

Grandmother snapped the quilt sharply until the edges lay out beyond Sophie's toes.

"Tell me the story again, Grandmother," Sophie begged.

"Which story would that be, my Sophie girl?" Grandmother sneaked a grin at the corner of her mouth. It was always the same story that Sophie asked for, night after night.

"The one about China Rooster!"

"Ohhhhh. That story. Well, it has been told for years that China Rooster lives in the hills and valleys of our land. And of all the spirits of the wild, he is the most sacred. For it is he who blesses the harvest and brings prosperity and health to our people."

"Where did China Rooster come from Grandmother?"

"It is said that the first China Rooster was once the protector of a great Chinese emperor. It was forbidden to touch the creature, by penalty of death. But one day, the emperor wanted to impress a maiden with his finery, so he bundled China Rooster off to the countryside where the maiden lived. There, the rooster felt the wind under his wings and gave sound to his voice. His spirit became unleashed and the rooster flew away from the emperor. The emperor was so angry that he forbade the rooster from ever returning to his kingdom."

"Then what happened to China Rooster?" Sophie breathed anxiously.

"China Rooster lived out his days in the valleys and woods of the country, and the people who lived there experienced great prosperity. Their crops grew double their normal size and their children were born strong and healthy. The emperor fell gravely ill, lost his power, and was never heard from again."

"Is that why we protect China Rooster on our land, Grandmother? Does he bring us health and prosperity, too?"

"We believe that, Sophie girl. Your ancestors have lived on and cared for this land for generations. And as long as the land has been treated with respect, and sacred areas have been left untouched, as the Great Spirit would have them, there has always been China Rooster. And we have prospered. Just look at *you*. You are a fine, robust little thing!"

"Oh, Grandmother!" Sophie giggled.

"Now, close your eyes child and sleep sweetly. There is work to fill our day tomorrow."

"Good night, Grandmother."

"Good night, Sophie."

Sophie rolled over and gathered the downy blankets up under her chin. In the distant night air she heard the raspy crow of China Rooster calling to his mate. Finally, her clucking answered him, and both voices whispered off into the darkness.

Not long after, strange men came to Sophie's home. They tried to persuade her family to sell their land so that more houses could be built. Sophie's family called a gathering and took a vote. They told the men no. Their land was all they had to pass on to the next generation. It provided for their health and their future. They would not sell.

The men were angry. They bought as much land as they could, all around Sophie's family's land. They tore down the trees. They dug up the fields and valleys. They filled in the streambeds and built roads. They stuck house upon house upon house, until they blocked out the sky. China Rooster could not be heard. China Rooster disappeared.

But Sophie's family stood strong by their land. They knew what would happen. They had seen foolishness before.

Winter came, and with it the heavy storms. Wind and rain streaked across the land where the houses grew. There was nothing to protect them from the elements. Roads flooded. The water grew too swift to stay within the border of the streets. It over-flowed into every house. The small, unnatural trees that were planted in concrete yards, snapped under the fierce winds and bitter cold. What little land was left, was ripped up and blown across the countryside. When winter stopped to catch its breath, the new "town" was gone.

Sophie's family had a difficult winter, too. But they had planned ahead, as always, and left sacred spaces with stream and wood and pasture, so that Nature could provide for herself and all her moods. Even so, they were saddened by the great loss all around them.

As spring warmed, planting proceeded as usual. But summer growth and fall harvest were only fair. Sophie's Grandmother became ill with a fever that no one had seen for generations. Finally, an elder from many towns away was called in for advice.

"I have seen this only once before. Tell me of your seasons. Has the land been good to you?" he asked Sophie's father.

"It has been only fair, Wise One," Sophie's father answered. "There was great tragedy here this winter past. The town that grew at the edge of our land destroyed much of the balance that Nature depends upon for her Winter Fury. As a result, our land, too, has been affected."

"And what of the China Rooster?" he queried.

"What?" Sophie's father looked puzzled.

"He is gone. He is gone Father!" Sophie replied to her father's confused expression.

"When he returns," the Elder said, "so will your Grandmother's health, little one. There is nothing that I can do except encourage you to trust the natural ways."

In the weeks remaining before winter, Sophie and her family built scrub shelters for China Rooster. They constructed nests and huts of twigs, brambles, and branches to provide security. They laid sunflower stalks along the edge of the woods and left crops to stand in the fields for protection. They prayed to the Great Spirit and waited.

Sophie tucked herself into her bed, since Grandmother could no longer climb the stairs to her room. She lay in the darkness and squeezed her eyes tightly closed, trying to remember what the song of China Rooster sounded like.

Krrok-`ook. Krrok-`ook. She barely recalled the sound.

Krrok-`ook. Krrok-`ook. That was it! That was the song of China Rooster. But had she heard it in her head or was it real? A second later, it repeated. *KRROK-`OOK. KRROK-`OOK!* Sophie sprang up and rushed to her Grandmother's bedside.

"Did you hear him?" Sophie practically exploded with excitement.

"I heard him," her Grandmother sighed. "And such a beautiful sound it was. Now sleep sweet, my Sophie girl. China Rooster has returned and all will be well very soon."

The following morning, Sophie ran to the kitchen. There, beside the stove, stirring her morning meal, was Grandmother.

"Then it's true! The story of China Rooster is true!" Sophie exclaimed.

"Did you doubt it, Girl?" her Grandmother looked puzzled.

"I thought it was only a story; an old ancestor's legend to put me to sleep with at night. I didn't think it could be real."

"Think less, Sophie, and listen to your heart more. It always knows the truth."

Grandmother hugged Sophie mightily and sat down beside her to give thanks for their food and good fortune.

THREE

THE PERFECT STEW

There was once a woman who thought she loved to cook…well actually, she loved to eat…so cooking was a necessity…but she thought how wonderful it would be to be a really *good* cook…and most of all, she wanted to be able to cook a really good stew…one that was healthy and hearty and made your insides feel warm and cozy on a cold winter night…one that all your friends couldn't wait to eat…a stew *so* delicious that it made your mouth water even thinking about it…a really good stew that could warm even the coldest spirit from the inside out… so she went to the bookstore and purchased a half dozen books on cooking…she took them home…read every single one of them from cover to cover…and set to work in her kitchen….cooking every single recipe in every single one of the books she had purchased… there were some strange recipes, indeed...but the woman thought that the best way for her to become a really good cook, was to cook every recipe she could possibly find...

after weeks of cooking and cooking and cooking…not one of the woman's dishes turned out…in fact, some of them were downright tasteless...and others were actually horrible…. completely discouraged, the woman thought that she had surely missed some important step along the way…something in the process that had escaped her…so back to the bookstore she went…and this time…the woman purchased a half dozen books on how to stock your pantry, set up your workspace, and organize your kitchen in order to be a good cook…and another dozen books with new and different recipes…

she read every single book from cover to cover…then set to work in her kitchen…she re-organized and de-cluttered and established a workspace…she stocked her pantry shelves with every imaginable item that could be used to cook with…then she began cooking and cooking and cooking… she cooked every single one of the new and different recipes that she read about in the new and different cookbooks… and still…even with all her study and all her effort…the recipes didn't turn out the way she wanted them to…and in fact, quite a lot of them were downright tasteless…

so the woman decided that there must be something that she was missing…. something that she hadn't learned yet that would help her to make the perfect stew…she pondered and pondered what she had done wrong…she nearly beat herself up with reproach…how could she ever learn to cook a really good stew when she couldn't even make a single recipe come out right? Finally, the woman decided to take a few days off from cooking and go to the beach…there she could re-evaluate just how important being able to cook a really good stew was to her…so she packed a suitcase…took a warm sweater and a bag for whatever treasures she might find… and headed west…the woman stayed in a small cottage near the beach…one where she had her own kitchen and a view of the breakers beyond…she strolled through the sleepy little village….past the bakery, the bookstore, the druggist, and the market…she kicked broken seashells along the sand with her bare feet....and she thought a lot about what she knew. She knew she loved to cook...she knew a lot about cooking...she had a great kitchen at home – a set-up any chef would be thrilled to have...she knew how to select good and healthy foods....so what was the problem with her being able to cook a really good stew? She had the foundation...the ideas...the experience... and as she sat there on the beach....watching the waves roll in and out....and the sun slowly crawl down behind the horizon-line...she knew in her heart that she could do it...she could make a really good stew....all she had to do was relax...trust her instincts and remember.......remember the smells...remember the tastes... remember the feeling of a really good stew... and then she would be able to make one herself.

So the next day, the woman strolled with purpose through the open air market... taking a pinch of that herb and a little bit of this vegetable... some of that meat....savoring the aroma of the stew in her mind....and when she returned to her little cottage she began to put everything together...she didn't need a recipe...she already knew everything she needed to know…she chopped and diced and cut and braised and simmered and stewed….and when the stew was finally done...she set a place for herself at the window, with the view of the breakers beyond…and she took a bite…*slowly*…savoring the experience with every sense possible…and the stew tasted good…really, *really* good…in fact, it was the most marvelous thing that she had ever tasted….and the woman was so very happy…she finally felt a sense that this stew was healthy and hearty …that all her friends couldn't wait to eat it…that it was a stew *so* delicious it made your mouth water even thinking about it…it was such a good stew that it would warm even the coldest spirit from the inside out on the coldest winter's night…and do you know what the woman did next?....she smiled and took another bite of the perfect stew.

FOUR

SIR GLENN OF THE FOREST

Once upon a time, in a land far, far away....there was a family...a not so extraordinary family...just a regular family with a mother, a father, and one child...a son.
Things became very difficult in the land where the family lived...and they were forced to leave their home...and travel a great distance...to find a new home...a new place where they could live and thrive. At night, as the son lay by the campfire trying to fall asleep...he could hear his parents arguing...and while he could not always hear all the exact words...he knew that they were very upset, and he felt that

much of their anger had to do with him. He wasn't sure what to do about this…so he stuffed the worry away…deep down inside…covered it up… and tried to be the best boy he could possibly be.

One day…when the sky was dark and heavy with storm clouds…the family stopped early to make shelter for the night…the boy was told to stay by the small rickety wagon that they drug alongside them, while the mother and father ventured out into the dark forest to gather wood and wild roots. Time crawled by like a 2-legged bug, and the sky grew darker and darker…and still the boy's parents did not return… soon the wind picked up and howled through the darkened forest like a pack of wild wolves….so the boy decided to crawl up into the wagon and pulled the canvas cover over his head…he was scared and cold…hungry and lonely…he had no where to go…and no one to cry out to for help…all he could do was hold onto himself and pray that he would awaken in the morning… to find his parents there by a crackling fire… with fresh meat for them to eat and a wild story to tell him.

But when daybreak came…there was no one there in the woods but the boy….when he finally gathered his courage enough to come out from under the canvas cover…all he could see were dozens, no maybe even hundreds, of fallen branches, and the ground looked as though it had be plowed for planting…but the sun shone brightly, if not coldly, in the harsh morning light.

The boy took the last few crusts of bread from the tin box his mother had packed and ate them slowly, hoping to make them last, or seem like more food than it really was… he tried to decide what he was to do…now that he was alone… a stranger in a strange land…and he did not even know what land it was.

The boy spent days constructing a shelter from the old wagon and exploring the area around him...he would count his strides away from camp on each outing...so that he could always find his way back to shelter and some sense of belonging. The forest was so dense…the boy could not establish a landmark or even see the sky enough to determine the time of day…to venture too far from his point of shelter could mean certain death…for the nights were cold and dangerous in the open air of the woods…and all he had to count on now was himself.

Weeks and months passed…though the boy was not aware of how much time had actually progressed…he spent his days searching for meager sustenance …and his nights huddled down like a kit in a burrow…cold, afraid, and with no companions except for a few woodland creatures….he could hardly remember what his parents looked like…it had been such a long time that he had been on his own…and he still could not find a way out of the woods because he was scared to move too far afield of his shelter…he felt so abandoned…and yet he survived.

Eventually…the seasons changed, and the days became longer and the nights more mild…the boy could go farther each day, because of the lingering light…and he was beginning to realize that only by going *beyond* his zone of comfort, would he ever stand a chance of saving himself.

Then one day...around midsummer…when the boy had traveled far from his base camp…he thought he heard voices…he was not sure for it had been such a long time since he had heard anything but his own mumblings, and the sounds of the forest around him. He sneaked over to a fallen tree and hunkered down behind it..and there in the near distance, was a sight the likes of which the boy had never seen before….there was a wagon...no, a coach…painted in bright colors and edged in gold…with two gleaming, glistening, black stallions pulling it… with harnesses of bejeweled silver…and standing just to the side of the coach was a women dressed in the most beautiful gown of silks and fur…his eyes could barely take in the whole spectacle. The woman called out to someone whom the boy could not see…and he was pondering on this when he was snatched from behind and lifted well into the air…his feet, dangling and squirming like a fish out of water…it was then that he heard his own voice coming back to him through his ears…"PUT ME DOWN! I AM A MAN AND YOU CANNOT TREAT ME THIS WAY!"

Almost instantly, the boy landed with a thud on the ground…and he turned to stare up into the kindliest face he had ever seen…the face was not young….no, in fact, it was quite aged….but one would never have known that by the man's strength…and there in the man's eyes, the boy saw laughter….not the way people laugh *at you* when you are a dolt or do something silly….but rather the laughter that comes with living a good life…the kind of life that lets you look at the world as a challenge to be enjoyed and entertained by…

"I beg your pardon, young sir," the man replied. "I did not intend to offend…only to offer protection to my wife from what I thought might be a roadside bandit." The old gentleman helped the boy to his feet and brushed the leaves and dirt from his torn dungarees.

"May I have the pleasure of knowing to whom I am speaking?" the older man asked. The boy, having been on his own and lost inside his head for so long, was dumbstruck for a moment…no name came out…in fact, no words came at all… as if they had completely frozen deep within his chest.

"Well, if you cannot offer me a name, perhaps I will have to call you Sir Glenn of the Forest, since that is where we have found you." The woman came forward now…and the boy could see, that she, too, was much older than he first thought, though still beautiful in her stature and demeanor…she took the cloak from her shoulders and wrapped it around the boy in a motion that almost made him weak in the knees…. given that it had been so long since anyone had taken care of him in such a manner.

The kindly old couple took the boy home with them…and not just any home… but to a stone castle on a hill that overlooked a thousand acres of forest that belonged to them…it amazed the boy to think that he had been lost in those woods all this time…with loving kindness and a home so very near…and yet a world away from the life that he was living.

Time passed, and the boy they named Glenn, grew into a man…indeed…and a fine man at that…he worked hard every day…he studied books and nature…he listened to petitioners from all over the kingdom and made fair and impartial judgments…and he developed a wonderful sense of humor and perspective about life and the ways of the world…and while he would occasionally sit and wonder... most often at night when he was all alone… what ever had happened to bring him to this point in his life…he never belabored the point, or felt sorry for what he might have missed…instead, he awoke to each new day and left the fear and loneliness behind him…and went out into the world to bring help and comfort to others, as he could.

At long last, the elderly couple called Sir Glenn of the Forest to their private chambers…and each embraced him as they would a son…

"You have been a complete blessing to us," they told him. "For when we were alone and without purpose, you came and gave us one. You have filled our lives with happiness and laughter, some sorrow, but many more joys. We are old now, and have no one to leave our kingdom to. We are hoping that you will accept our home as yours and be a steadfast steward to all who reside here."

The boy…now a grown man, looked at the two old faces in shock and horror. Suddenly, that small frightened boy, way down inside of him, sprang forth and cried out,

"No! You cannot leave me. I am too young and small and afraid to be on my own. You must stay and take care of me and tell me what to do. How will I ever grow into a man…into a real man…without you?"

"Whatever are you talking about?" the old woman asked. "You *are* a man…in fact, in all the ways that matter, you have *always* been a man. Do you not remember the day we found you, wandering in the forest? You told us then that you were a man…and you were right. Why, you had been taking care of yourself for many, many months…making choices and decisions to direct your life…and while you might have felt lonely…you were never alone…the universe was there, all around you…protecting you and teaching you how to live and grow and be…You have no further need of us to help you do that…*you have done that for yourself all along…*"

"And besides," added the old man, "We aren't dying yet…we will still be around to laugh and talk and live and love you…we only want you to know that the work that you have done, seemingly for others all these years, has now paid its reward…it is time for YOU to recognize what WE have always seen….you are a strong and wise and loving spirit, who did not allow his ***beginning*** to become his ***ending…***You have made a good place for yourself in the world, despite how you came to be here…you are the bravest of souls and the most compassionate of beings…because you understand on the inside how it feels to have to save yourself…to make positive choices for your life…to listen to your inner voice and *be guided by that which is deep down inside you."* "Fear?" the boy asked. "No…*not fear* my son," the old man chuckled … "LOVE. You have been guided by love... whether you knew it or not...you have always been guided by love...and that is a noble gift indeed."

And so it was that Sir Glenn accepted the couple's offer and led the kingdom with peace and compassion for many years to come. And every once in a while he would reflect back on the words that the old man had spoken to him...the words about making choices for himself, despite his poor beginnings...about his time of being lonely in the forest, yet *never* alone... about listening to his inner voice...and he was knew it was so.

FIVE

AN IDEAL GARDEN

And that reminds me of the story of the woman who wanted to be self- sufficient…to provide for herself…to be in control of her own destiny… so she decided to plant a garden…she got together all the usual accoutrements – the shovel, the hoe, the organic fertilizer, the stakes and twine…then she went to the nearby farmer's market to pick up the seeds to plant in her freshly tilled plots…she came home with a large jar filled with a variety of seeds that the local farmer assured her would grow every vegetable she could possibly need to be self-sufficient…squash, corn, cucumbers, eggplant, chard, lettuce, carrots, broccoli, melons, even tomato seeds and herb seeds…the woman eagerly planted the seeds in the warm fertile earth, watered them, and waited for time and Mother Nature to bring her the garden of her dreams…

As harvest time neared….the woman became evermore anxious to reap the benefits of her work… but, lo and behold…when she went to the garden and began sifting through the foliage….and digging through the mounds of earth….all she found was radishes. Radishes! Red ones, yellow ones, purple ones….but all radishes! The woman was astounded – how could all her hard work yield only radishes? And she hated radishes!

So she returned to the farmer's market stand and reported to the local farmer what had happened. The farmer was quite surprised and handed the woman another jar of seeds to replace the first one…with the reassurance that surely this time, she would grow the garden of her dreams…

When spring came...the woman eagerly anticipated the day when she could plant the new seeds out into the warm earth…water them...and wait for time and Mother Nature to bring her the garden of her dreams…

And when harvest time arrived….and she began sifting through foliage…and digging through mounds of earth…all she found was radishes! Radishes…again! Red ones, yellow ones, purple ones…but all radishes! This time the woman was quite upset. She had done *everything* she thought she should do and *still…* she got back only radishes! She stomped off to the farmer's market and gave the old farmer a piece of her mind. The farmer was so distraught that he gave the woman TWO jars of seeds this time, and at no charge… encouraging her that certainly, THIS TIME…everything would be quite different and she would grow the garden of her dreams…

So when spring came, the woman did everything *JUST as she had done BEFORE*….with the same care and precision and inward determination that, surely, ***this time, things would be different.***

But at harvest time, all she found in her garden was radishes! AGAIN! This was the last straw…She must be the very *worst* gardener in the entire world…for how could she plant an entire garden of vegetables and end up with only radishes? Time and time again? That was it. She was *never* going to plant another garden…*neve*r be self-sufficient…*never* be able to provide for herself…She was a *failure*!

Then one day, not long after… she was out for a walk and happened by the home of a wise old woman…the old woman carried a basket over one arm and pruning shears in the other hand and was filling her basket full of the most beautiful, lush, and tasty-looking fruits and vegetables imaginable….the woman could not help but stop to admire the garden and the old woman's incredible bounty.

"You must surely be the world's greatest gardener ever," the woman said to the old crone as she neared the fence line…

"Nonsense!" came the crone's reply. "I have just *learned* from the mistakes that I made early-on… and *adapted* to the environment around me. Then, all my efforts, along with a little support from Mother Nature…paid off in this glorious bounty you see all around us. You see…with a garden…as in life…you cannot plant the same seed over and over again…and expect a different harvest…nature is ever-changing…always adapting…never rigid…you must be flexible and learn to go with the flow…"

Then the old crone handed the woman a huge, ripe peach plucked fresh from the branch hanging overhead…It was the most delicious fruit the woman had ever tasted…full of earth and sky and wind and water….effort and love and hope….

All the way home, the woman thought about what the old crone had said…Of course! It finally made sense! *With a garden…as in life…you cannot plant the same seed over and over again and expect a different harvest…you cannot do the same thing and get a different result…*

So all winter long…the woman gathered together every seed and gardening catalog she could find…perused them with great care…determined which species…which variety…would grow best in *her* garden…and made a *new* plan…

Then, the following spring, she tilled the soil, added compost and organic fertilizer to sustain the growth… and planted all *new* seeds… with effort and love and hope…

And what do you suppose she harvested *that* fall? You know it – She harvested the garden of her dreams…at last!

SIX

ATTITUDE IS EVERYTHING

I once knew a man named Jess. Jess was a great guy…the kind of guy that everybody likes and wants to be around. I worked with him for a time right after college when I was selling heavy machinery…we worked for a huge wine manufacturing and marketing company…with a number of different lines of products…we didn't actually work in the same division…but Jess was company-renown…he was always in a good mood, no matter what the day brought…if another employee was down or depressed, Jess would be there….telling them to look at the bright side of the situation…he was a natural motivator, and yet he never came off preachy…

One evening after work, while talking over a beer…I finally decided to ask Jess why he was always so positive… "You can't really be feeling so positive ALL the time…so what gives? How do you do it? And even more…WHY do you do it?"

Jess smiled at me and said, "You know…I wake up each and every morning and I know that I have two choices I can make…even before I set a foot on the floor…I can choose to be positive or I can choose to be negative…I can choose a good mood or I can choose a bad mood…now, what do I really have to gain by choosing a bad mood?" He chuckled. "So, I choose a good mood and a positive outlook. I know that every time something bad happens, I can choose to be a victim…or I can choose to grow stronger and learn from the experience. I choose to learn and grow."

"But what about all the people around you who are always whining about their poor lot in life?" I asked him.

"Well, with them, too…I can choose to listen and accept their whining and complaining, or I can reframe it for them… and point out the positive side of life…how they can find the lesson and the good things worth living for."

"You make it sound so easy but it's not," I huffed.

"Sure it is," he replied. "Life is all about choices. We *all* have free will. We all make hundreds of decisions every day…heck, maybe even every minute….it's all about choice…if you strip away all the other stuff…all the drama…all the could-a/would-a/should-a's…… it always comes down to how YOU react to a situation….not the guy next to you…but **YOU!**....Bottom line….you choose to be in a bad mood or good…to let other people affect you or not…it's your life and it's your choices that *make* your life."

We finished our beers and said goodnight. Not long after…I left that job and moved on to another career, but I reflected on that conversation the rest of that evening, and for many weeks afterward…I thought about what Jess had said and I tried to apply it to my own life…to make a conscious choice for the positive…. rather than just reacting to whatever life threw at me…sometimes I even had good results…

Many years later, I ran into a mutual colleague of Jess' and mine and asked after him. The friend said that Jess had fallen off a large piece of wine manufacturing equipment while on a sales call, and had been crushed in the machinery. He was air-lifted to the hospital and after 20 hours of extensive surgery and weeks in intensive care and rehab…he had been released…his spine had been fused in two places…he had lost one leg in the accident, and had to wear a brace to stabilize his remaining leg…what a tragedy, I thought…..

Unexpectedly…I ran into Jess a few months later…"Jess!" I exclaimed upon seeing him. "How are you?" I immediately regretted having asked that question.

"I'm great!" Jess replied with enthusiasm. "Couldn't be better," he beamed.

"How can you say that …after everything that happened to you, Jess? Weren't you terrified you were going to die? What went through your mind when you got hurt?"

Jess smiled that effusive smile of his and said, "Well…the first thing I knew, once everything stopped moving and I realized I was in a precarious situation, was that I had two choices: I could choose to die…or I could choose to live…So, I chose to live!"

"But weren't you scared you wouldn't make it in time?"

"Well, the emergency crews were really great…they were with me almost immediately and they kept telling me over and over…that I was going to make it...I was going to be fine…and the helicopter crew was fantastic…the entire flight to the hospital…they kept saying..hang in there buddy…you're gonna make it and be just fine…but then…when they wheeled me into the emergency room, and into the operating suite, and I saw the fear on the faces of the medical staff…I knew I had to take action…I *had to shift* the tide of their gloom and doom right away…in their eyes, I was a dead man already."

"So what did you do?" I asked Jess.

"Well…there was this one, big, burley male nurse named Brent, who tried real hard to be busy and not make eye contact with me…so when he finally asked me if I was allergic to anything, I replied 'Yes'…and everyone in the room stopped for a moment to hear what I was going to say...so I took a deep breath and yelled out… 'WINE!'

Well, everyone roared with laughter…and when the room quieted again I told them that I was still alive and I was choosing to stay that way…and they were to go into my surgery with the same expectation…that I would live through it all!"

And he did….thanks to the skill and dedication of his medical staff…the love and support of his family and friends….but mostly, because of his positive outlook and attitude toward life…

Everyday…we have the choice to live fully, or to let life get us down….I guess I learned from Jess that attitude is everything…to live life fully, and make each and every day count for something positive.

SEVEN

GATHERING WOOL

Once upon a time – not so very long ago – people wandered their fields and pastures all day…keeping their animals safe from harm – watching the seasons flow gently into one another – gathering the bits of wool from the stones and bushes the sheep had brushed alongside – rescuing those small tufts of fluff that would otherwise go to waste… they would add them all together to make a sweater for warmth… or maybe even a blanket to curl up beneath…and yet, to be branded as one who is "gathering wool" has become a negative thing – a "not doing" thing – synonymous with day dreaming and laziness and sloth.

Which actually brings to mind a girl I once knew named Sarah. She was what some might call a "free spirit" – she never worried much about how life would turn out…only that it would turn out. I remember people calling her flaky, and an air-head, and often accused her of gathering wool – all because she was calm and never really seemed to stress out about anything. But Sarah always accepted these labels with a quiet, sort of Mona Lisa smile…she took them as a compliment…because to her…they meant that the world would take care of her…would provide for her needs…she would just calmly gaze off to the horizon…living in the moment…free to experience the beauty around her that other people always seemed to miss…always remaining mindful of the abundance there is in nature and the world, rather than the lack…quite like the parable of the lilies of the fields or the birds so free and unfettered…not tied down and yet always cared for by some higher power…simply trusting…knowing…being…more A PART than *apart* … more inclusive than exclusive…easy to bend with the breeze and never break…giving over to go with the flow…even when it occasionally means altering course…greeting the sun, the rain, the wind… as friends rather than foes…what has always been…and will always be…

And Sarah seemed to know all of this, maybe more…. somewhere deep inside of her…never fought to sway opinions or change minds…what would be the point of that…while others felt it was their duty to label her "silly", or "lazy", "un-informed", and maybe even "stupid" for not making lists and stacking stones… or setting aside seed for the future…she was calm and quiet and sure…and she always landed on her feet…just like the proverbial cat with nine lives…knowing but not *knowing,* there is a greater plan in play…knowing but not *knowing,* everything is as it should be…it will be okay…and everything will always work out for the best.

I wonder at all the sleepless nights we might avoid if we had the same outlook on life as Sarah…if we could approach life more as one gathering wool…oh, that the joy could be multiplied and spread…if we would only *know* that we already *know* everything we need to *know*…when we quiet ourselves…look around…look within….for we already have all the answers…we just need to gather a little more wool to draw them out.

EIGHT

MAYBE…MAYBE NOT

Once upon a time…you may know that there was this ancient Chinese fable about a man who had good luck and bad luck…but it was really all about his perspective on those events that make the story. Maybe your very wise mind can figure out the ending to this tale, then.

I heard of a man who lived alone. He was not a happy man, nor was he a sad man, either. He just was. One day, his alarm clock failed to ring in time to awaken him for work. When he stepped out on his front porch to pick up his morning newspaper, his neighbor remarked on the man's bad luck, since he had obviously missed his train and would be very late for work. "Maybe…Maybe Not," was the man's only reply.

While the man was back inside finishing his breakfast, a knock came at the door. He opened it to a dozen or more people with balloons, and signs, and flowers, claiming him to be the new winner of a million dollar prize. "Since you were home to answer your door you have just won the entire jackpot!" the microphoned lady exclaimed. "Aren't you just the luckiest man alive?" "Maybe…Maybe Not," the man answered.

The following day, the news of the man's financial windfall hit the airwaves, the newspapers, and the internet. Media vans were parked on his front lawn. Old acquaintances and friends and family he didn't even know he had, called him at all hours of the day and night. The man, used to a life of peace and quiet, was now inundated with every sort of person, who seemed to feel that *only he* had that something that would make their lives meaningful. A co-worker mused, "It must be nice to feel so special and so needed, especially since you have been so alone in the world." To which the man replied, "Maybe…Maybe Not."

Now, since this was a very large sum of money, the man decided to invest it. He did his research and made his selection, and put all of the winnings into an investment portfolio. A few months later, the bottom dropped out of the market and the man lost all of the funds he had invested, with the exception of a small sum that he held out for a rainy day. "Wow! What a bad investment you made," said some. "Maybe…Maybe Not." "How wise you were to hold some of it back," said others. "Maybe…Maybe Not."

Quite quickly though, all those "new" friends and acquaintances, and the media vans, and all the rest, vacated his yard and quit calling him for advice and company. "How sad," said his barber. "To be left alone again after the joy and spotlight of having so many people around you." "Maybe…Maybe Not," said the man, as a small smile played around the edges of his mouth.

So you see…not everything is as it appears to be on the surface. One man's junk is another man's treasure. It is always about how we each interpret a thing…how we assign a value to it. And sometimes, a wise person will choose to gain a greater perspective before determining the value of an experience. It May-Be… or it May-be-Not.

NINE

COLORING OUTSIDE THE LINES

I once knew a girl, a long time ago, when we were just small children…she was always drawing or painting or putting together those little models called dioramas…she was so creative…leaves became gowns for a princess…pebbles became a castle for ladybugs…she could capture the fuzzy veil of a cloud on a piece of bark painted with watercolors…it was as though the wheels in her mind were always creating…always looking for a new view through which to see the world.

Even when we were in kindergarten, we all knew Christina would be an artist…was an artist already! So, when we entered elementary school, the teachers had already heard of Christina's talent…they were interested…supportive…and pleased with the art she created…even if sometimes it was a little bit…how should I phrase it? Different? Avant-garde? Weird? They humored her and let her have her way.

But by the time we reached high school, the teachers were not so supportive…and less than pleased when Christina chose to interpret their lessons in her own artistic bent. They became angry – she became moody…they ridiculed and reprimanded her for being different – so she searched for more ways not to fit it…it was a trying time for everyone, but mostly for Christina…because a truly creative spirit *cannot – should not* – be broken, at any cost…anyone can color inside the lines…it takes little thought and even less creativity…but it takes someone *truly confident* in themselves…and in their own expression of life…to be willing and able to draw *outside the lines…* to go where no one else may have thought to go, or been brave enough to take that step into the unknown.

I lost track of Christina over the years…I heard that she had taken a job selling copies of other people's artwork…I heard she was unhappy…unfulfilled…I knew that those words spoken so long ago were stuck inside her heart, and had locked her artistic spirit deep inside…like a prisoner in one of her pebble castles.

Then one day, not so very long ago, I saw a program about progressive new artists, and who should be there but Christina…she was glowing…lit from within…you could see her radiating with joy…as were the people surrounding her….all of them loving her designs and her art…the announcer even went on to say that Christina had a number of wealthy patrons backing her, and was going to have an original piece hung in the Museum of Modern Art…what a far cry from the shackled young woman I had known in high school! In the end, the announcer asked Christina the secret to her overnight success….she replied, wistfully, that nothing comes to us overnight – it takes many long hours and many lonely nights to realize our success…but mostly, she said, her success came from being true to herself…listening to her inner voice…knowing who she wanted to be, and what she was meant to create here on earth…then never letting anyone or anything cause her to stray from that path…she acknowledged there were some rough years…and some years when the path took crazy twists and turns…but in the end, she realized, this is who she was meant to be…it was inside her all along…and these are her gifts to share with the world…and aren't we all the luckier for it.

TEN

CHOP WOOD, CARRY WATER

Once upon a time, and not so very long ago, there was a woman. This woman was not so young…but not so old, either…she was really quite at the mid-point of her life…at a crossroads…which is part of the problem, you see…the woman was recently widowed and was so disarmed by this trauma…that she couldn't move…not forward…not backward…not even sideways…

Now, she had always prided herself on being able to handle anything that came her way…good, bad, no matter…. she was the cool one…the one who calmly collected her wits and went ahead with whatever needed to be done…but it was different this time…half of her was gone now…and the half that remained could not think…or process…or make a plan, or even a list…oh, she was a great one for lists! She just sat…day after day…staring out her window into nothing much at all…and when her thinking processes surfaced… which they did from time to time…she tried to remember what it was that she should be doing…somewhere inside her head…she must know what she should do.

Then one night, while she was lying alone on her big empty bed…she heard a small, sweet voice, nearly whisper in her ear… "chop wood, carry water"…the woman sat up and turned on the lights to see if someone was there… but she was still alone…then she heard it again… "chop wood, carry water"…she recalled hearing her great grandmother speak those words when she, herself, was no more than a toddler…but she never knew what they meant…and what's more…she never really cared to find out.

Suddenly…she understood the meaning and the intent of the simple phrase, "chop wood, carry water"…just for today…you do what you most need to do…to stay warm…to stay alive…to deal with what is immediately in front of you and will serve you for the next few minutes…then you do it again…and again…and again…before long…your wood pile is stacked high…and your well is full once more.

When the woman awoke the next day…she followed the whispered advice she'd received in the nighttime shadows like it was her mantra…soon, the trauma eased…the numbness receded…the pain – though always present – stepped to the back of her heart…instead of where it had been…front and center, and on a collision course with destruction.

Many, many days of chopping wood and carrying water passed…seasons came and went…but the woman started to feel again…to feel better again…to find hope and promise in the rising sun…the first buds of spring…the migration of the geese overhead…Life goes on…we can step aside from it for awhile…but as she learned…we must always remember to step back up on the carousel and ride the painted pony once again.

ABOUT THE AUTHOR

Shawn Marie Howe started out in life as a writer of stories. While most kids were at the swimming pool or off riding bikes, she could be found sitting at her antique writing desk, giving flight to her imagination by penning poetry and stories of faraway places.

She studied to become a nurse, which led to the development of a holistic outlook on health and wellness. She departed from the bedside and took up herbalism, hands-on healing, and hypnosis. Today, she runs a holistic healing practice for those searching for alternatives to allopathic medicine.

Shawn Marie lives in Oregon with her husband, daughter, and a farmyard of friendly critters. She enjoys gardening, making stained glass, and of course writing. This is her first volume of *Metaphor Stories for Hypnosis: Stimulate Change While Telling A Tale.*

Made in the USA
Charleston, SC
18 July 2011